WHY DO I VOMIT?

✦ and other questions about digestion ✦

Angela Royston

www.heinemann.co.uk/library
Visit our website to find out more information about **Heinemann Library** books.

To order:
 Phone 44 (0) 1865 888066
 Send a fax to 44 (0) 1865 314091
Visit the Heinemann Bookshop at www.heinemann.co.uk/library to browse our
catalogue and order online.

First published in Great Britain by Heinemann Library, Halley Court, Jordan Hill, Oxford
OX2 8EJ, a division of Reed Educational and Professional Publishing Ltd. Heinemann is a
registered trademark of Reed Educational & Professional Publishing Limited.

OXFORD MELBOURNE AUCKLAND JOHANNESBURG BLANTYRE
GABORONE IBADAN PORTSMOUTH NH (USA) CHICAGO

Designed by Joanna Sapwell and StoryBooks
Illustrations by Nick Hawken
Originated by Ambassador Litho Ltd
Printed in China by South China Printing Company

ISBN 0 431 11072 7
06 05 04 03 02
10 9 8 7 6 5 4 3 2 1

British Library Cataloguing in Publication Data
 Royston, Angela
 Why do I vomit?.– (Body matters)
 1. Vomiting – Juvenile literature
 I.Title
 612.3'2

Acknowledgements
The Publishers would like to thank the following for permission to reproduce photographs:
FPG: 21; Gareth Boden: 4, 6, 9, 12, 15, 19, 20, 22, 24, 25, 26; Popperfoto: 23; Science Photo Library: 11, 13,
17, 18.

Cover photograph reproduced with permission of Tudor Photography.

Our thanks to Anne Long for her help in the preparation of this book.

Every effort has been made to contact copyright holders of any material reproduced in this book. Any omissions
will be rectified in subsequent printings if notice is given to the Publisher.

CONTENTS

Words printed in **bold letters like these** are explained in the Glossary.

WHAT HAPPENS TO THE FOOD I EAT?

When you swallow a mouthful of food, it passes down a tube into your stomach. There it is churned around and broken up into smaller pieces. It then passes into your **intestines** – a long tube that joins your stomach to your anus. On the way, the food is broken down into smaller and smaller pieces. Most of these very small pieces pass through the walls of the intestines into your blood. The rest is waste, and it leaves your body when you go to the toilet.

As this girl swallows a mouthful of her sandwich, the food begins a long journey from her mouth through her digestive tube.

Breaking up food

Food, such as cheese, bread, eggs and fruit, contains the chemicals your body needs to survive and grow. But your body cannot use the chemicals as they exist in the cheese, bread or tomato. Each food consists of several different chemicals, some of them combined together. The food has to be broken down into separate substances, or building blocks. This process is called digestion.

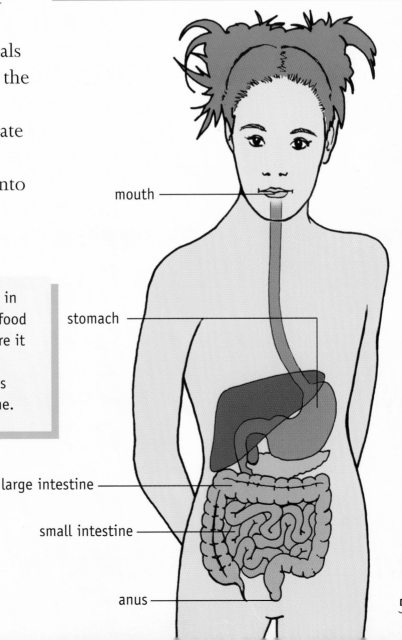

Digestion

The body has several ways of breaking down food. First, the teeth grind it up so that it mixes with saliva, then the stomach mashes it around, like a food mixer. Special chemicals called **enzymes** attack the particles of food and break them into separate building blocks. The building blocks pass into the blood.

The digestive tube begins in the mouth and takes the food to the stomach. From there it passes through the small intestine. Waste food goes through the large intestine.

THE DIGESTIVE SYSTEM

The length of the digestive system from the mouth to the anus is more than five times as long as your total height. In an adult it is about 9.5 metres (31 feet) long.

mouth

stomach

large intestine

small intestine

anus

5

WHY ARE TEETH DIFFERENT SHAPES?

You have two rows of teeth. Those in the upper jaw work against the teeth in the lower jaw to break up food – the first step in the digestive process.

Teeth are different shapes because they have different jobs to do. Between them they break food into smaller pieces and so begin the process of digestion. Each kind of tooth has a name. The flat front teeth are called incisors. The pointed teeth behind them are the canines. The large, flat-topped teeth at the back of the mouth are molars.

A mouthful of teeth

Each tooth in your upper jaw is matched by the same kind of tooth in your lower jaw, and you have the same kinds of teeth on each side of your mouth. When a baby is born, its first set of milk teeth are already formed in the gums. As these teeth push through the gum, a second set, called permanent teeth, form below them. As a milk tooth falls out, it is replaced by a permanent tooth.

Incisors and canines

You have eight incisors, four in your upper jaw and four in your lower jaw. They are flat and sharp and slice through food like knives. You use them to bite into fruit and other solid food. Behind the incisors, you have four sharp, pointed canine teeth, one at each corner of the front of your mouth. They pierce food, such as meat, and grip it while you tear off a bite.

HARDER THAN BONE

Your teeth are coated with a layer of enamel – the hardest substance in the body. Below the enamel is dentine which is as hard as bone.

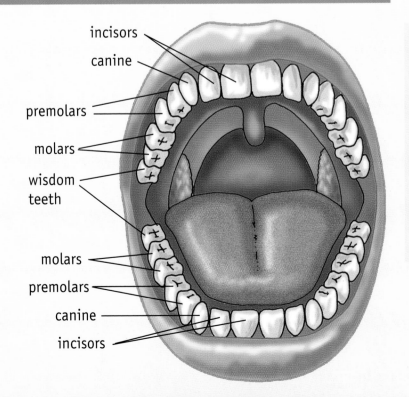

incisors
canine
premolars
molars
wisdom teeth
molars
premolars
canine
incisors

A complete set of permanent teeth. Milk teeth do not include all the back teeth, and the wisdom teeth only come through when you are about 18 years old or older.

Molars

Behind each canine are two flat-topped premolar teeth in adults which grind up food. Behind the premolars are the molars. They are larger and bumpier than premolars so that they are even better at grinding up food.

Mouth-watering

You cannot chew up food with just your teeth. You need your tongue to push the food around your mouth. As you chew, saliva mixes with food and makes it mushy and easy to swallow.

Swallowing

When the mouthful of food is mushy enough, the tongue pushes it to the back of your mouth. As soon as it touches the soft palate at the start of your throat, you automatically swallow. Special flaps close off the tubes to your nose and lungs so that you cannot breathe in air as you swallow.

The tongue takes the food to the back of the mouth and pushes it down the throat.

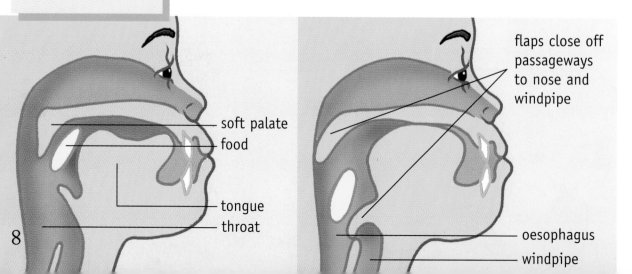

soft palate
food

tongue
throat

flaps close off passageways to nose and windpipe

oesophagus
windpipe

Down the tube

The mouthful of food slides down the **oesophagus** into your stomach. The walls of the oesophagus close in behind the food and push it down, just like squeezing a tube of toothpaste. This means that you do not have to be upright to swallow food, but can swallow even when you are lying down. The walls of the oesophagus are covered with **mucus** to help the food slide down.

This boy pushes the bar out of the wrapper bit by bit as he eats it. The food travels down his oesophagus in a similar way.

CHOKING

Sometimes a crumb goes down the wrong tube. It goes into the windpipe, which leads to the lungs, instead of into the oesophagus. Coughing usually pushes the crumb out, sometimes with the help of a pat on the back.

9

HOW BIG IS MY STOMACH?

Your stomach stretches when you eat. A child's stomach can hold about half a litre of chewed up, mushy food. An adult's stomach holds about one litre. This may not sound very much, but food becomes less bulky when it is chewed up. Bread, for example, is mostly air.

Bands of muscles move the food in different directions.

oesophagus

valve

outer wall

valve

food

small intestine

muscle

Inside the stomach

The inner wall of the stomach is covered with many tiny pits. At the bottom of each pit is a **gland** that makes gastric juice – a strong acid that helps to kill off any germs that you may have eaten with the food. It also helps to break down food. Between the outer and inner walls is a layer of strong muscles. They stir the food, squeeze it and mash it into a purée, called chyme.

FOOD IS MOSTLY WATER

vegetables:	about nine-tenths water
potatoes:	four-fifths water
rice:	about two-thirds water
chicken:	two-thirds water

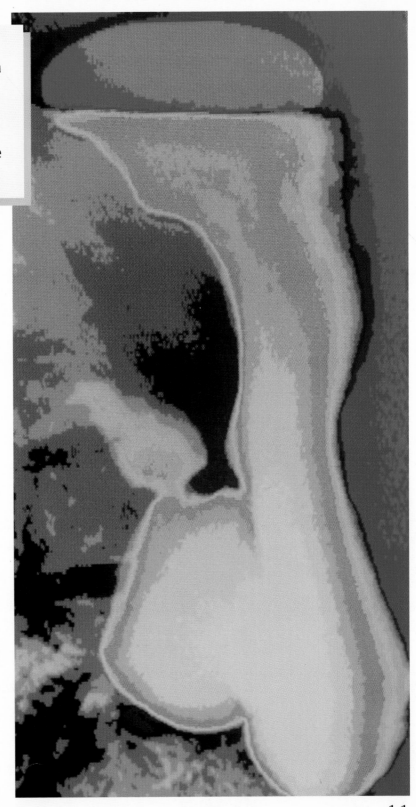

The stomach is shaped a bit like a boxing glove. This is what the inside of your stomach looks like when it is empty.

Stomach valves

A **valve** is a device that allows something to move only in one direction. The valve at the top of the stomach stops food moving from the stomach back up the **oesophagus**. Food stays in the stomach until it has been mashed into chyme. A valve at the bottom of the stomach opens from time to time and a squirt of chyme passes into the small **intestine**.

WHY DO I VOMIT?

You vomit when your body needs to get rid of the contents of your stomach fast. Vomiting protects you mainly from germs and poisons. The acidity in the **gastric** juices can kill many germs, but not all. If you have swallowed food that has too many germs for the gastric juices to kill, you will be sick. When some food goes bad, it produces poisons that may make you sick. The box opposite shows some of the things apart from food poisoning that can make you vomit.

This boy has eaten some food that does not agree with him. He will feel better when he has vomited.

Forced out

When you vomit, the **diaphragm** pushes down on the stomach, forcing it to heave the unwanted food back up the **oesophagus** and out through the mouth. The food is pushed violently the 'wrong way' through the **valve** at the top of the stomach. Sometimes the valve relaxes by mistake and a small amount of the contents of your stomach comes back up your oesophagus. This gives you a burning feeling and a nasty taste in your mouth, but you are not actually sick.

Burping

Burping is when the valve at the top of the stomach opens to let gas out. Some foods produce more gas than others. Drinking fizzy drinks is very likely to make you burp.

Rough seas make some people seasick. The movement of the boat disturbs the liquid in their ears and their sense of balance.

THINGS THAT CAN MAKE YOU SICK:

- bad smells, particularly the smell of vomit
- illnesses such as scarlet fever or gastric flu
- migraine
- food allergy
- being anxious
- motion sickness, due to travelling in a car, bus, aircraft or boat
- rich food
- alcohol and other drugs.

HOW LONG DOES FOOD STAY IN MY BODY?

Most food stays in your body for 16 to 24 hours. It takes about 5 seconds for a mouthful to slide down the **oesophagus** to the stomach, but it will probably stay there for about 4 hours. The mushy food then passes a squirt at a time into the small **intestine**. Here the useful parts of the food are slowly digested. It takes about 5 hours for the rest of the food to pass right through the small intestine to the large intestine. Its progress slows down here and it may be 7 to 16 hours later before undigested food finally leaves the body. Some food can take even longer.

The small intestine and the organs that supply it with digestive juices. Digested food passes from the small intestine into the blood.

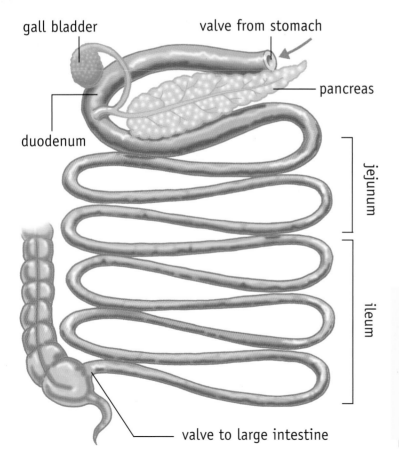

gall bladder

valve from stomach

pancreas

duodenum

jejunum

ileum

valve to large intestine

The small intestine

The small intestine consists of three parts – the duodenum, the jejunum and the ileum. The duodenum is as long as twelve widths of your fingers. In adults this is about 20 to 25 centimetres. Food stays in the duodenum for about an hour. While it is here it is mixed with digestive juices from the walls of the intestines and from the pancreas and gall bladder.

Bile works like washing-up liquid. It breaks up fat into tiny droplets.

Digestive juices

Tubes from the pancreas and gall bladder feed into the duodenum and spray the chyme with digestive juices. The juice from the pancreas mixes with the chyme and neutralises the strong acids made by the stomach. The gall bladder stores a bright green liquid, called bile, which is made by the liver. Bile breaks up globules of fat into smaller droplets that are easier for the body to digest.

Enzymes

Digestive juices contain several different **enzymes**. Enzymes are special chemicals that attach themselves to large, complicated **molecules** and break them up into smaller, simpler molecules that can be digested. The enzyme itself is not digested. After it has broken up one large molecule it floats away and attaches itself to another large molecule.

The villi

The wall of the small **intestine** is lined with millions of tiny villi. They look like tiny fingers sticking out from the wall of the intestine. Together they give the inner wall of the intestine a huge area for food to pass through. They are only about 0.5 mm long but are packed close together, like the bristles of a brush. Their walls are so thin that simple molecules pass through them into the blood. The blood, now rich with food molecules, is taken straight to the liver.

The villi are filled with tiny blood vessels. Simple food molecules pass through the walls of the villi into the blood.

villi

blood vessels

The liver

The liver is the largest and one of the most important organs in the body. It takes food from the blood and stores some of it until it is needed. Then it releases the food into the blood.

OTHER THINGS THE LIVER DOES:

- filters waste and poisons out of the blood
- changes poisons into harmless substances
- sends poisons and waste to the kidneys
- produces a substance that helps blood to clot
- destroys dead red blood **cells**
- produces bile.

This person is suffering from jaundice, an illness of the liver. The skin looks yellow because there is too much bile in the blood.

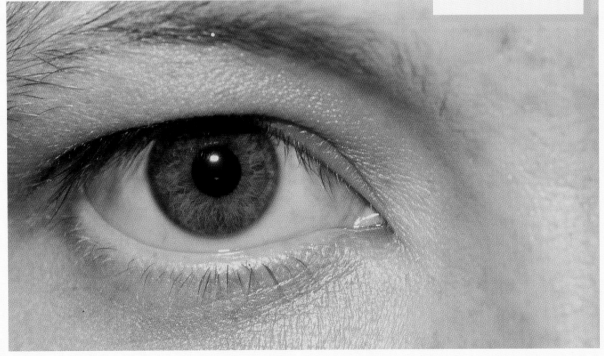

WHAT HAPPENS TO UNDIGESTED FOOD?

The large intestine is about 1.5 to 2 metres long. It makes a large loop around the coils of the small intestine.

Undigested food passes from the small **intestine** through a **valve** into the large intestine. As it passes through the large intestine, water and **vitamins** and **minerals** are absorbed into the blood and the mushy paste slowly turns into soft solids, called **faeces**. Faeces are stored in the rectum at the end of the large intestine and leave the body when you go to the toilet.

The large intestine

The large intestine gets its name because it is wider than the small intestine, but it is actually much shorter. It consists of the colon, the rectum and the anus. A mushy paste of waste food moves very slowly through the colon.

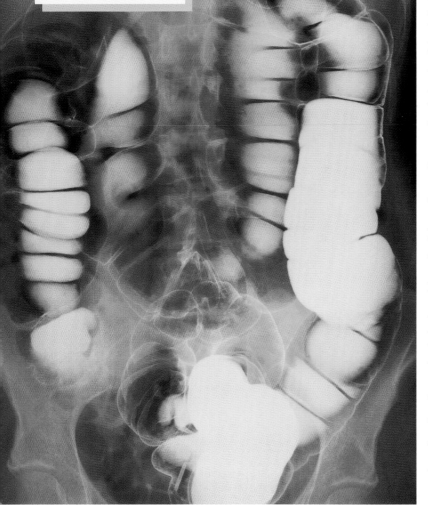

Undigested food

Undigested food consists of **fibre**, the hard parts of fruit, vegetables and grains that the digestive juices cannot break down. It is mixed with digestive juices, water, **bacteria**, dead **cells** from the lining of the intestines and **mucus**. Left-over bile gives faeces their brown colour. The more fibre the paste contains the easier it is for the colon to move it through.

Bacteria that live harmlessly in the large intestine can make you ill if they get into your stomach. It is important to wash your hands after using the toilet.

Water

Water with minerals dissolved in it moves through the walls of the colon into the blood. Not all the water is absorbed, however. About three-quarters of faeces is water. It helps the faeces pass smoothly out of the body.

Bacteria

Bacteria in the large intestine make certain vitamins that the body needs. They pass through the intestine walls and are absorbed into the blood. These bacteria also produce the gases that make faeces smell bad.

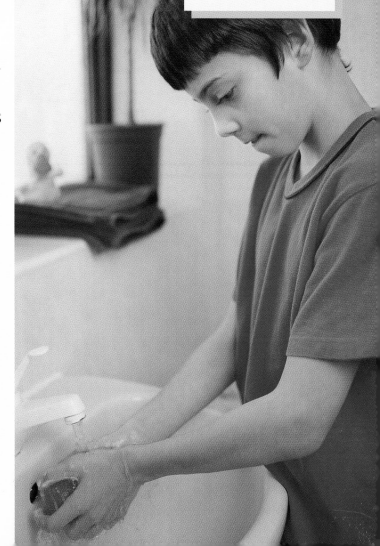

WHY DOES MY STOMACH RUMBLE?

Your stomach rumbles when you are hungry. It is letting you know that your body needs a new supply of food.

Your stomach rumbles when it is empty. The muscles in the stomach wall contract and squeeze, but the only thing in your stomach is digestive juice. It is the sound of the digestive juice whirling in your empty stomach that makes the rumbling sound.

Feeling hungry

A rumbling stomach is a sign that you are probably hungry. You also feel hungry when the amount of sugar in your blood falls. Feeling hungry makes many people irritable, but, more important, it makes you want to eat. Your body needs a regular supply of different kinds of food.

Why we eat food

Food gives us the nutrients (parts of food that the body uses) that our bodies need to survive. Most food is turned by the body into energy. Every living **cell** in the body needs energy to do its job. Other nutrients make new cells. Most cells last only a few days or a few months. Dead cells have to be replaced and children need to make millions of extra cells as they grow. Food also provides many of the special chemicals your body needs to stay healthy.

Different kinds of food

The three main kinds of nutrients are carbohydrates, fats and proteins. Carbohydrates and fats give you energy. Proteins give you energy too, but, more important, they help to make new cells. Fat also helps to keep you warm. In addition, the body needs small quantities of important chemicals – **vitamins** and **minerals**. Many foods contain a mixture of nutrients. Cheese, for example, contains protein, fat and several vitamins.

Everything you do uses energy which your body gets from food. Food gives you all the nutrients you need to be healthy.

Carbohydrates

Carbohydrates include sugar and starches. Potatoes, rice and anything made with flour, such as bread and pasta, are rich in starch. During digestion **enzymes** break down the starch into simple sugars. Carbohydrates are the first foods to be digested.

If you chew a mouthful of bread for a long time, it begins to taste sweet. The enzymes in your saliva have changed some of the molecules of starch in the bread into sugar.

Digesting carbohydrates

Enzymes in your saliva start to break down starch into sugar. Enzymes in the stomach carry on the work and some sugar is absorbed into your blood through the walls of the stomach. Sweet things such as fruit, sweet drinks and chocolate contain sugar which is quickly absorbed through the stomach. Starches take longer to digest and so give you a longer-lasting supply of energy. Most starch is digested and absorbed in the small **intestine**.

Proteins

Fish, cheese, milk, meat, eggs and soya beans are all rich in proteins.

Other kinds of beans, lentils, nuts and flour also contain some protein. Proteins begin to be broken down in the stomach, but they are mostly digested in the small intestine.

Fats

Fats are among the last foods to be digested. Bile from the gall bladder breaks large globules of fat into tiny droplets. Enzymes then break the droplets into the smaller **molecules** of fatty acids and glycerol. These are mainly absorbed in the ileum, the last part of the small intestine.

This tennis player is eating a banana to keep his energy level up. Starch is a better source of energy than pure sugar. Sugar gives a quick rush of energy that leaves you feeling more tired afterwards.

ENERGY FROM FOOD

Energy is measured in calories. Ten-year-old children need about 2000 calories per day.

Portion of baked beans	170 cal
Small packet of crisps	154 cal
Portion of cornflakes	110 cal
Small tin of tuna	105 cal
Boiled egg	90 cal
Slice of bread	about 60 cal
1 teaspoon of sugar	15 cal

DO I REALLY NEED TO EAT GREEN VEGETABLES?

Green vegetables contain **vitamins**, **minerals** and plenty of **fibre**, all of which your body needs to stay healthy. You can get these things from other foods, such as fish and cheese, but vegetables – particularly raw green vegetables – are a rich source. Provided you eat a wide range of foods, you should get all the minerals and vitamins you need.

Vegetables like these are rich in vitamins, minerals and fibre.

Vitamins

Vitamins are special chemicals that your body needs to work properly. They are mainly known by letters of the alphabet. If you do not get enough of any vitamin, your body will suffer. If you do not get enough Vitamin C your gums may begin to bleed. The body makes some vitamins itself. Vitamin K is made by **bacteria** in the large **intestine**.

Minerals

Minerals include the chemicals calcium, iron, potassium and sodium. The body uses calcium to build strong bones and teeth. Iron is needed to manufacture red blood **cells**. If your body is low in iron, you will become **anaemic**. Potassium and sodium are also needed for healthy blood.

Fibre

Fibre is found in vegetables, fruit, wholemeal bread and pasta. The stalks of vegetables, for example, are rich in fibre. Fibre adds extra bulk to the mushy paste that becomes **faeces** and makes the large intestine work better. If your diet does not contain enough fibre, you are likely to become **constipated**.

FOOD RICH IN VITAMINS AND MINERALS:

vitamin A	milk, leafy green vegetables, eggs
vitamin B	fish, whole grain cereals, yeast, vegetables
vitamin C	fresh fruit, vegetables, potatoes
vitamin D	eggs, oily fish, margarine
vitamin E	olive oil, vegetable oil
vitamin K	leafy green vegetables
calcium	milk, cheese, green vegetables
iron	meat, bread, vegetables
potassium	fish, meat, fruit, vegetables
sodium	most foods, table salt

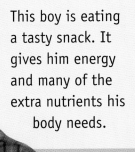

This boy is eating a tasty snack. It gives him energy and many of the extra nutrients his body needs.

WHY DO I GET THIRSTY?

The best way to quench your thirst is to drink a glass of water, but every kind of drink consists mainly of water.

You get thirsty when your body becomes short of water. The body loses up to 3 litres of water every day – through sweating, in urine and **faeces**, and in your breath when you breathe out. Adults need to drink about 2.5 litres of liquid a day to replace all the water lost. The rest comes from the water in food.

Made of water

About two thirds of your body weight is due to water. Apart from body fluids such as blood, saliva, tears, **mucus** and urine, every other part of your body, including muscles, bones and skin, also contains water. Even before you feel thirsty, you may get a headache and find it difficult to concentrate when your body becomes short of water. You feel thirsty when the lack of water makes your mouth and throat dry.

Water balance

All the liquids you drink contain water and so does much of the food you eat. It is absorbed into the blood mainly through the walls of the large **intestine**. As the blood passes through the kidneys, they filter out urea (waste poison made in the liver) and any extra water and salts. In this way, the kidneys clean the blood and control the amount of water in the body. Urine is water with urea and salts dissolved in it. It is stored in the bladder until you urinate.

The kidneys filter the blood and remove extra water with urea and extra salt dissolved in it. It trickles down into the bladder where it is stored as urine.

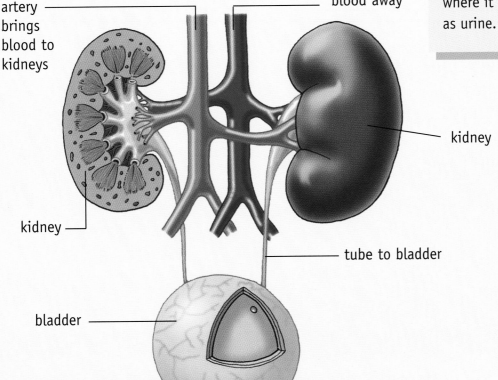

artery brings blood to kidneys

vein takes filtered blood away

kidney

kidney

tube to bladder

bladder

IS EATING FAT BAD FOR ME?

Fat itself is not bad for you, provided you do not eat too much. Your digestive system breaks fat down into fatty acids, which the body needs to grow new **cells**, and glycerol. The problem is that too much fat makes you fat because any extra is stored as fat under the skin. The 'Balance of Good Health' plate shows which foods you should be eating most and least of.

This plate of food shows how much you should eat of different kinds of food. If you follow it, you will achieve the 'Balance of Good Health'.

Balance of Good Health

Scientists who study nutrition have put different kinds of food into five groups. They say that about a third of the food you eat should consist of starch such as bread and cereals. This will give you plenty of energy. Another third should consist of fruit and vegetables. You need to eat some protein and dairy food, but not too much. And you should only eat a small amount of fatty and sugary food.

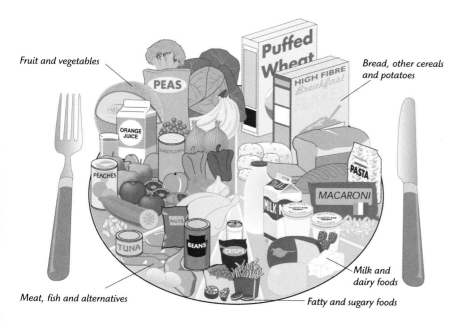

Fruit and vegetables

PEAS

ORANGE JUICE

SWEETCORN

PEACHES

Puffed Wheat

HIGH FIBRE Breakfast

Bread, other cereals and potatoes

PASTA

MACARONI

MILK

TUNA

BEANS

CRISPS

Milk and dairy foods

Meat, fish and alternatives

Fatty and sugary foods

BODY MAP

saliva in mouth

oesophagus

liver

gall bladder

stomach

pancreas

large intestine

small intestine

rectum

anus

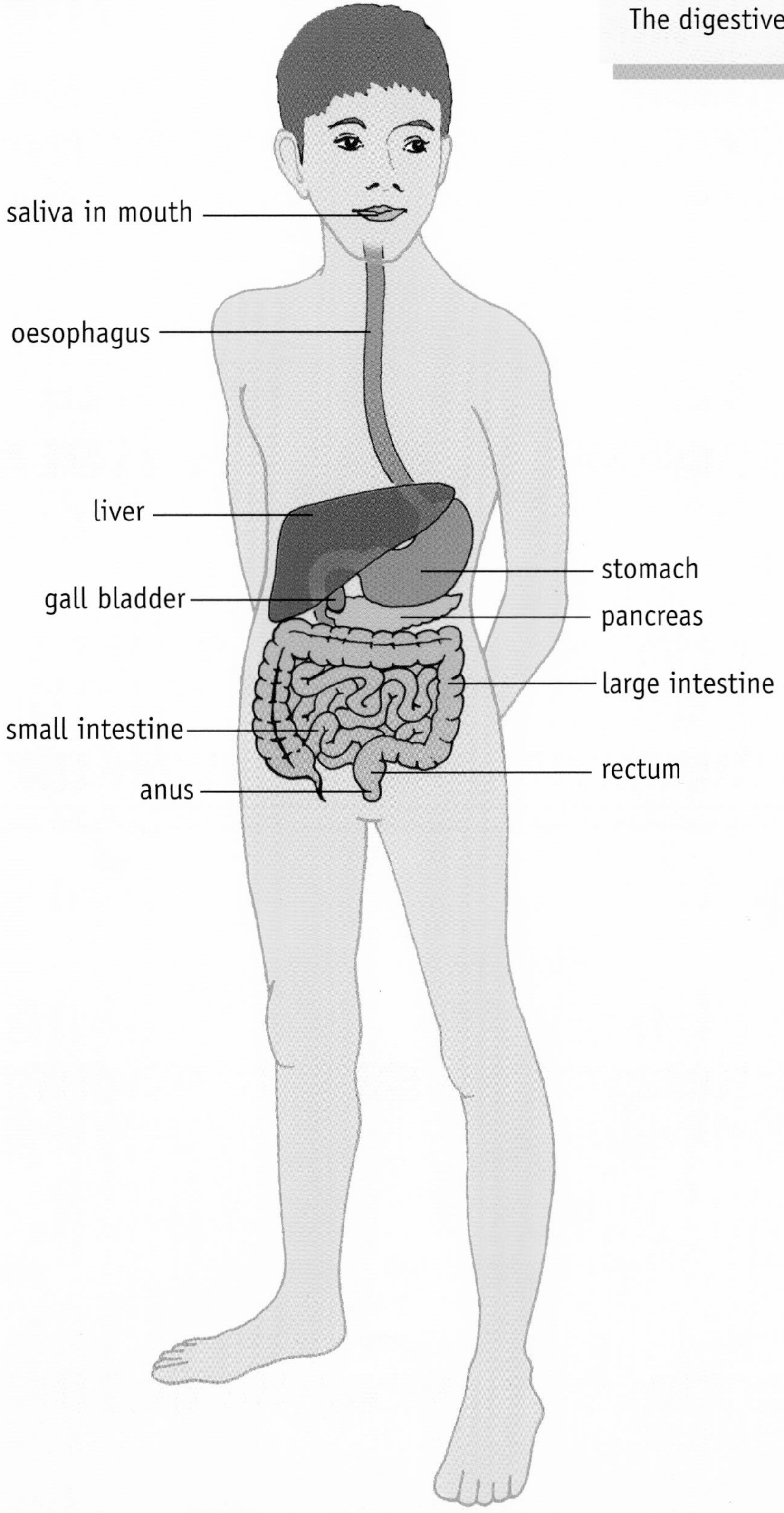

GLOSSARY

anaemic   an illness that makes you feel weak and tired. It is caused by a lack of iron in the blood.

bacteria   tiny living things. Some kinds of bacteria are germs that cause disease.

cell   the smallest building block of living things. The body has many kinds of cells, including skin cells, blood cells and cells that make the intestines.

constipated   when the faeces are too dry to pass easily out of the body

diaphragm   a sheet of muscle between the lungs and the belly

enzymes   special chemicals that break down food so that it can be digested

faeces   solid waste that leaves the body when you go to the toilet

fibre   the hard parts of fruit, vegetables and grains which the body cannot break down

gastric   to do with the stomach

glands   parts of the body that produce particular substances such as sweat and saliva

intestine   the long tube that food passes into after it leaves the stomach

mineral a chemical found in rocks and soil. The body needs several minerals that it gets from the food you eat.

molecule the smallest particle that makes up a substance

mucus a slimy liquid produced by the lining of the nose, bronchial tubes and other parts of the body

oesophagus the tube that joins the throat to the stomach

valve a device that allows liquid or gas to flow in one direction only

vitamins chemicals found in food that your body needs to stay healthy

FURTHER READING

Body works: Eating, Paul Bennett, 1998, Belitha Press

Look at your body: Digestion, S Parker, 2001, Franklin Watts

INDEX

Titles in the *Body Matters* series include:

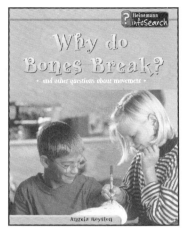

Hardback   0431 11075 1

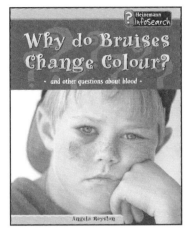

Hardback   0431 11073 5

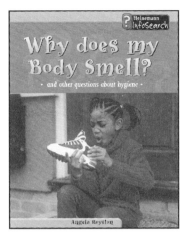

Hardback   0431 11077 8

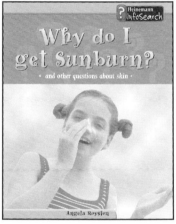

Hardback   0431 11078 6

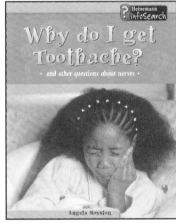

Hardback   0431 11076 X

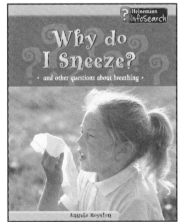

Hardback   0431 11070 0

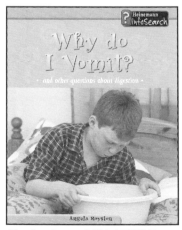

Hardback   0431 11072 7

Hardback   0431 11071 9

Find out about the other titles in this series on our website www.heinemann.co.uk/library